MINDFUL COLORING

Book for Adults & Teens, Vol. 1
A Journey To Boost Your Confidence
Motivational & Self-Love Messages

THIS BOOK BELONGS TO:

_____

_____

K.G. Carmen

PUBLISHER

—— EST 2023 ——

Created in the United States of America

First Printing, 2024

ISBN 979-8863738376
ASIN B0DH4QR917

amazon.com/author/kgcarmen

SCAN TO SHOP

Size: 8 in x 10 in
(20.32 cm x 25.4 cm)
110 Pages | Coloring Book
Soft Paperback Glossy

Mindful Coloring, Vol. 1
A Journey To Boost Your Confidence

Reno, Nevada
XVI.CB2.20230809

Dedication

In heartfelt tribute to mommylove, Irene,

Like your favorite flower, the exquisite stargazer lily, your beauty shines brightly. Just as this flower stands tall and proud, your strength and grace have illuminated our lives.

May the colors that will grace these pages reflect the vibrancy of your love, and may your spirit continue to bloom as beautifully as the stargazer lily.

With much love and gratitude,

Kei

A Message From the Author:

Thank you so much for purchasing Mindful Coloring, Vol. 1: A Journey To Boost Your Confidence. Your support allows me to pursue a dream that stemmed from self-discovery and inspirations.

If you enjoyed this book and want to help others find it, please post a review on Amazon! Kindly follow my author page at *amazon.com/author/kgcarmen*, or scan the QR code located on the back cover, to view more products and receive new release updates.

It will bring me so much joy to see your masterpieces! Please share your work, tag @kgcarmenpublisher and use #kgcarmenpublisher.

I am so happy that you chose to join me on this journey! Always remember to be kind to yourself and others.

with love,

Keigie xo

SCAN HERE TO
RATE THIS BOOK

  @KGCarmenPublisher

Share your coloring art whether it is a work in progress or an finished masterpiece!
#KGCarmenPublisher on social media

The back of each coloring page is black to prevent coloring materials from bleeding through to the other side of the page. Please use a backing page, typically a blank sheet of paper, to help absorb any excess ink and prevent ink transfer to the surface beneath the coloring page.

Self-love

The practice of valuing and caring for oneself. It involves recognizing your worth, treating yourself with kindness and respect, and prioritizing your well-being. Self-love encourages positive self-talk, setting healthy boundaries, and nurturing your physical, emotional, and mental health. It is essential for personal growth and overall happiness, fostering a positive relationship with yourself.

Breathe

Embrace the present moment and let your creativity flow with this mindful coloring book. Immerse yourself in the soothing strokes of color as you find tranquility and joy in each page. As you fill in each thoughtful design, find a sense of peace and relaxation wash over you, allowing stress and worries to fade away. This is your time to relax, unwind, and connect with your inner artist. Take a deep breath, pick up your favorite coloring tools, and lose yourself in the meditative practice of mindful coloring. Whether you spend a few minutes or a few hours, each session offers a chance to nurture your creativity and enhance your well-being. Happy coloring!

In the garden of your heart, self-love is
the most beautiful bloom.

Love yourself like your life depends on it, because it does.

Embrace your uniqueness with a
heart full of love.

You are worthy of all the love
you give to others.

Nurture your spirit with acts of self-love.

Self-love is the key that unlocks
your true potential.

Your worthiness shines through self-love.

Treat yourself with the kindness you deserve.

Self-love is the foundation for a fulfilling life.

Your love for yourself is a
masterpiece in progress.

Cultivate self-love like a precious garden.

With each stroke of self-love, you paint your own masterpiece.

Celebrate the love that resides within you.

Cherish yourself with the same
love you offer the world.

Self-love is a journey, not a destination.

You are enough, and your self-love is a gift.

Radiate self-love and watch your light shine.

Nurture your soul with self-love.

Your self-love is the compass
guiding you to happiness.

Embrace self-love as your superpower.

You are a masterpiece of
self-love and charm.

Practice self-love and watch
your world blossom.

Self-love is the greatest gift you
can give to your soul.

Choose self-love and watch your
world transform.

Believe in the power of YOU.

Thank you!

As you close the pages of this book, may you carry the sense of calm and creativity it has brought you into your everyday life. Gratitude fills my heart for your dedication to self-care and artistic expression. Remember, the colors you've chosen reflect the beauty within you. Keep coloring your world with mindfulness and joy.

Lots of love,

K.G. Carmen

"If you hear a voice within you say 'you cannot paint,' then by all means paint, and that voice will be silenced." – Vincent van Gogh

Thank you for your support. Kindly follow my author page to receive new release updates. If you enjoyed this book and want to help others find it, please post a review on Amazon!

**SCAN HERE TO
RATE THIS BOOK**

Visit *amazon.com/author/kgcarmen* to view more products, or scan the QR code located on the back cover.

 @KGCarmenPublisher

Share your coloring art whether it is a work in progress or an finished masterpiece!
#KGCarmenPublisher on social media

K.G. Carmen
PUBLISHER
— EST 2023 —

65717149R00064